7.95

ENGLISH

Antony Miall
David Milsted

Xenophobe's Guides

Published by Xenophobe's® Guides

Telephone: +44 (0)20 7733 8585
E-mail: info@xenophobes.com
Web site: www.xenophobes.com

First printed 1993
New editions 1999, 2008
Reprinted/updated 1994, 1995, 1996, 1997,
1998, 1999, 2000, 2001, 2002, 2003, 2004,
2005, 2006, 2007, 2008, 2009, 2010, 2011
2012, 2013, 2014

Editor – Catriona Tulloch Scott
Series Editor – Anne Tauté
Cover designer – Jim Wire & Vicki Towers
Printer – CPI Antony Rowe, Wiltshire

ePub ISBN: 9781908120304
Mobi ISBN: 9781908120311
Print ISBN: 9781906042295

Contents

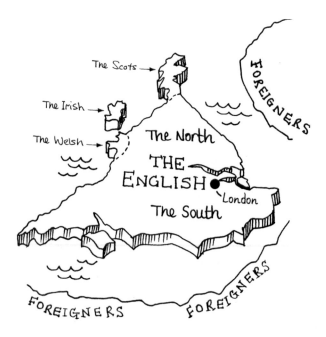

The English have an instinctive distrust of the unfamiliar and nowhere is this more clearly seen than in their attitude to the geography of their own country.

The English population is 53 million compared with 3 million Welsh, 6 million Irish (North and South combined), 4 million Kiwis, 5 million Scots, 22 million Aussies, 65 million French, 81 million Germans, 142 million Russians and 315 million Americans.

England is five times larger than Sicily, but could fit into France five times.

Nationalism & Identity

Forewarned

The attitude of the English towards other nations is not so much xenophobia (fear of foreigners) as xenopili (pity for foreigners for having the misfortune to be, well, NOT English). As Cecil Rhodes (who gave his name to Rhodesia – today's Zimbabwe) once observed: 'To be born English is to win first prize in the lottery of life'. It is hardly surprising, then, that the English should feel a bit sorry for all the runners-up.

> **To be born English is to win first prize in the lottery of life.**

The last invasion of England was perpetrated 900 years ago by the Normans. They settled, they worked hard, they tried to integrate and fit in, they tried to share their wisdom and experience with the locals. They failed. The English did what they do best. They ignored the funny cooking smells, the unfamiliar clothes and peculiar accents and set about the long, slow, arduous task of turning the invaders into Englishmen. It took centuries of course, but it worked. 'Norman' is no longer a name redolent of invasion and locking up one's daughters: it is a quintessentially English first name.

The Venetian Ambassador, Andreas Trevisano, visiting London in 1497 made the following observation about the English:

'They do not believe that there are any other people than themselves, or any other world than England: and whenever they see some handsome foreigner, they say, 'He looks like an Englishman,' or, 'What a pity he is not English.'

These days the English are not as unanimous in this view as they once were, some regarding England as a place to escape from at every opportunity, but the majority remain innately mistrustful of 'abroad' – dodgy food, dodgy water, dodgy plumbing, and, worst of all, dodgy foreigners.

> **"The majority of the English remain innately mistrustful of 'abroad' – dodgy food, dodgy water, dodgy plumbing, and, worst of all, dodgy foreigners. "**

Geography reinforces this belief as the inhabitants look out to the sea all around them from the fastness of their 'tight little island'. Nobody would ever question the aptness of the newspaper headline: 'Fog in the Channel – Continent cut off.'

This insular mind-set is what you are up against. It is useless to imagine that you can succeed in penetrating it when so many have failed. But since the English take a perverse pride in acknowledging a total lack of understanding of foreigners, it would be gratifying to gain a tactical advantage by understanding them.

How they see themselves

The English see themselves as law abiding, courteous, tolerant, decent, generous, gallant, steadfast and fair. They also take pride in their self-deprecatory sense of humour which they see as the ultimate proof of their good nature.

Though they put themselves down in public, in their heart of hearts they believe the English to be superior to all other nations, and are convinced that all other nations secretly know that they are. In a perfect world, the English suspect that everyone would like to be more like them.

> **❝ In a perfect world, the English suspect that everyone would like to be more like them. ❞**

The English are convinced that the best things in life originate in England or have been improved there. Even their weather, though it may not be pleasant, is far more interesting than anyone else's, and is always full of surprises.

They are also convinced, with some justification, that no-one really understands them. In the words of one of their much loved song-writers, Michael Flanders:

'The English are moral, the English are good,
And clever, and modest, and misunderstood.'

This claim to be misunderstood is not to be seen as a plea for understanding. They do not want to be

3

understood – such intimacy would be an invasion of their privacy.

How they think others see them

The English are dimly aware of foreign criticism but feel it should not be taken too seriously. They are used to being seen as stereotypes and prefer it that way: they don't mind in the least that England is seen as peopled by bowler-hatted city types, football hooligans, silly-ass nobility and cheeky cockneys, all meeting in an ancient pub for a pint of warm beer.

> **66 They are used to being seen as stereotypes and prefer it that way. 99**

How others actually see them

Mostly they are seen as a relic of the glory days of the past when they were major players in the European sport of empire building.

They are also perceived as hidebound, prejudiced and unco-operative – a people who live in a land of costume dramas, shrouded in grey skies, sustained by fried sausages.

Foreign residents come to respect the English for their refusal to make a fuss and their adherence to personal principles, but remain forever bewildered by their uncomplaining attitude towards the shoddy and the second-rate, and see their concern with manners

4

as a substitute for personal style. The emphasis on table etiquette alone is a mystery in a country of people who are more than a little challenged in matters culinary.

How they would like to be seen

The English pride themselves on their sense of fair play, and rather assume that it is recognised and generally admired by all. They would like to be loved and appreciated for what they see as their sterling qualities. These attributes, which they bring selflessly to the world forum, include a reflex action which leads them to champion the underdog and treat persecutors with a firm hand, truthfulness, and a commitment never to break a promise or to go back on their word. Foreigners are expected to understand that if an Englishman hasn't kept his word, there is a very good reason for it.

> **66** Foreigners are expected to understand that if an Englishman hasn't kept his word, there is a very good reason for it. **99**

If possible, try to find it in your heart to be charitable about these and other beliefs, even if you believe them to be delusions. Aside from anything else, the moment you disagree with their vision of themselves, most English will take your side and agree with you. Respect for the underdog, you see.

How they see each other

Nowhere is the English people's instinctive distrust of the unfamiliar more clearly seen than in their attitude to the denizens of their own country.

Since time immemorial there has been a North-South divide in England. To the Southerner, civilization ends somewhere around the Watford Gap (just north of London). Beyond that point, he believes, the inhabitants are all ruddier in complexion, more hairy, blunt to the point of rudeness, and obsessed with stew – all of which he generously puts down to the cooler climate.

> **When it comes to their neighbours in the British Isles, the English are in absolutely no doubt as to their own predominance.**

In the North they caution their children with tales of the deviousness of the inhabitants 'down South'. They point to their softness, their fussy food and their airy-fairiness on all matters of importance.

Nevertheless, *any* English person no matter how hairy or soft, is entitled to special treatment. You only see faults in people you care about so, in a way, this continual criticism of each other is actually a display of affection.

When it comes to their neighbours in the British Isles, the English are in absolutely no doubt as to their own predominance. This they see as no petty prejudice but rather as a scientific observation. The

Irish are not to be trusted because they are too feck-less, the Scots are not to be trusted because (though clever) they are too careful with money, and the Welsh are simply not to be trusted.

However, the Irish, the Scots and the Welsh should take heart. To most of the English they are not quite as foreign as their cousins across the Channel. They should also remember that 'foreign-ness' for the English tends to start at the end of their own street.

How they see others

The English do like many individuals who are foreign since they generally know at least one foreigner who is almost 'one of us'. But there are very few nations they either trust or take seriously. Take the French. The French and the English have been sparring partners for so long that the English have developed a kind of love-hate relationship with them. They love France: they love its food and wine and thoroughly approve of its climate.

> 66 The English have a subconscious historical belief that the French have no right to be living in France at all. 99

They have a subconscious historical belief that the French have no right to be living in France at all, to the extent that thousands of English try annually to turn areas of France into little corners of Surrey.

However, the actual French are perceived as a bit

too excitable for any people with ambitions on the world stage. It is thought that a few more decades of English influence would improve them no end.

With the Germans the English are less equivocal. Germans are regimented, far too serious, and inclined to bullying; they have not even the saving grace of culinary skill. The Italians are too emotional; the Spanish cruel to bulls; the Russians are gloomy; the Dutch solid and sensible; the Scandinavians, Belgians and Swiss, dull. All oriental peoples are inscrutable and dangerous. The Indians, Pakistanis, Bangladeshis and Sri Lankans are put in a special category: they play cricket.

> **&& The Indians, Pakistanis, Bangladeshis and Sri Lankans are put in a special category: they play cricket. 99**

The rest of the world the English see as a playground: a series of interlocking peoples, customs and cultures all of which can be enjoyed, used, or discarded as the whim takes them. Their own experience has taught them to expect the worst of any situation, be pleasantly surprised if it doesn't happen, and slightly gratified with their own sensible misgivings if it does.

Special relationships

There are several favoured nations with whom the English feel a special affinity. They have close ties with the Australians, despite their disconcerting lack of restraint, the Kiwis, who have model manners but an annoying tendency to thrash them at rugby, and the Canadians, who elicit sympathy for being weighed down by permanent snow and being constantly mistaken for Americans.

The English like Americans. They like their 'can do' attitude, and their open natures. In many ways they would probably like them even more if only they didn't insist on being quite so... well... *American*. Deep down, the English regard Americans as English people who turned into something else as the result of an unfortunate misunderstanding, and who would be a lot happier if they just had the sense to turn back again. Then they could start talking 'proper' English.

> **❝ The English like Americans. They like their 'can do' attitude, and their open natures. They would like them even more if only they didn't insist on being quite so... well... *American*. ❞**

The English watch the participants on American television 'confess-it-all' shows with fascinated disbelief. They blame falling standards in their own cultural life on American influence, despite being hooked on their television sitcoms and series.

Americans have money and power and that makes any relationship special. But a smug feeling will always remain that having a history that goes back a bit further than the day before yesterday is a sign of a superior culture.

Character

Individualism

Whoever called the English 'the Island Race' only got it half right. Every English person is his or her own island. Only wars unite the English, and over the years they have become quite good at them. But natural modesty demands they should always look like losing until just before the end. It makes victory that much sweeter, and really annoys the loser.

English island mentality takes the form of a well-developed sense of individual personal freedom. They are fond of their rights, especially the right to privacy and the right to preserve one's personal space. This is an area surrounding each individual, which it is not good manners to invade.

> 66 People will leave a step between themselves and the next person on an escalator even when it's crowded. 99

English people will leave a step between themselves and the next person on an escalator even when it's crowded, or a vacant seat between themselves and their neighbour in the cinema, even when they know that in due course they are certain to be asked to move along to make more room. This has nothing to do with a morbid fear of body odour, it is more an extension of the 'an-Englishman's-home-is-his-castle' belief. Think of it as an invisible moat. Learn to shake hands at long distance.

Keeping a stiff upper lip

This characteristic pose involves keeping the head held high (pride), the upper lip stiff (to avoid the visible tremble which betrays emotion), and the best foot forward (determination). In this position, conversation is difficult and intimacy of any kind almost impossible. But it portrays the presence of that attribute which the English were traditionally expected to project – absolute self-control.

> **66 The stiff upper lip portrays the presence of that attribute which the English were traditionally expected to project – absolute self-control. 99**

It is acceptable to show one's feelings at football matches, funerals, or when welcoming home someone thought to have been dead. At all other times the English find a display of emotion disconcerting, though it is more acceptable if the perpetrator looks suitably embarrassed afterwards.

In recent years, however, there have been an increasing number of public occasions at which the English have allowed themselves to become positively Mediterranean.

Moderation

Moderation means a lot to the English, even to those who are incapable of moderate behaviour themselves. No matter how they behave personally, they share a fundamental dislike of anyone else behaving in a manner that 'goes too far'.

'Going too far' in polite society means displaying an excess of emotion, getting hopelessly drunk or cracking off-colour jokes and then laughing at them immoderately.

Creating a scene in public is altogether unacceptable. The English consider that anyone who does so is automatically in the wrong, even if they are actually in the right.

> **The admired way to behave in almost all situations is to display a languid indifference.**

The whole business of making a fuss has its own vocabulary, guilty parties being said to be creating a 'to do', a hullabaloo, a palaver, a kerfuffle, a song and dance – all of which are seen as socially undesirable.

When confronted by a disturbance in a public place such as a bus, English people will mostly duck down behind their newspapers and pretend it isn't happening. Extreme outbursts, such as road rage or football hooliganism, will incur a chorus of disapproval. Despite such behaviour being quite common, it is still perceived as un-English.

The admired way to behave in almost all situations is to display a languid indifference. Even in affairs of the heart, it is considered unseemly to show too much enthusiasm.

Paradoxically, the sentence 'This time you/he/she/they have gone too far' is the unmistakable prelude to a great deal of immoderate behaviour on the part of the speaker, who will then undoubtedly go too far him- or herself.

Two-facedness

With their emotions buttoned up and their composure in place, the English present a reassuring consistency to each other and the world at large. Underneath this calm exterior, however, there seethes a primitive unruliness which they have never quite been able to master. Climate has a lot to do with it. Heat waves bring out the beast in the English. Cold and drizzle calm them down.

There is an illogical relationship between the head and the heart. English people are capable of admiring something without enjoying it, and enjoying something they suspect is fundamentally reprehensible.

> **66 Underneath this calm exterior there seethes a primitive unruliness which they have never quite been able to master. 99**

Such two-facedness in the English character prompts the most common criticism of them – that they are hypocrites. They certainly appear to be, but appearances can be deceptive. The English believe that even the truth has two sides.

Attitudes & Values

Common sense

Common sense is central to the English attitude to almost everything in life. It is just plain common sense to carry an umbrella in case of rain. It is common sense not to sit on cold stone (which can give you haemorrhoids). It is common sense to wear clean underwear in case you are run over and taken to hospital. True to the maxim of the Boy Scouts' creator, Baden Powell, the English consider it common sense to 'Be prepared' at all times.

> **66 To fall foul of changing circumstances is inexcusable. Every plan for an outdoor event will have its indoor alternative. 99**

To fall foul of changing circumstances is inexcusable. Every plan for an outdoor event will have its indoor alternative in case the worst comes to the worst. Even accounting systems have a line for 'Contingencies'. The fact that when they sit down to a business meeting the English are more likely than any other nation not to be prepared for it does not deter them from believing that common sense will usually prevail.

Not showing off

Even if you have conquered the Atlantic in a small boat, if you are English you are expected to say no more of your achievement than to murmur: 'I do a little sailing from time to time.'

To force English people to trumpet their accomplishments or, for that matter, to show off your own is to make them feel uncomfortable. But should you subtly indicate that you are aware of their achievements, or admit that you have dabbled a bit yourself, they will modestly acknowledge the praise and enquire after your accomplishments.

Minding your own business

English people believe in minding their own business. Few outsiders understand how deeply ingrained this belief is.

The queue is one of the few places where the English allow themselves to talk to each other without having been formally intro-

> **66 The queue is one of the few places where the English allow themselves to talk to each other without having been formally introduced. 99**

duced. The other places are when taking the dog for a walk, or the scene of any serious catastrophe, like an accident. However it needs to be firmly understood that any friendships made in such circumstances must remain outside with the dogs, or stop when rescue arrives. Being trapped with a group of English people in, say, a train in a tunnel, might result in community singing, even the exchange of confidences, but it is not an invitation to more permanent intimacy. When, after such an experience, English people say: 'We really must meet again' – you are not meant to believe it.

A good sport

If an English man or woman refers to you as 'a good sport', you will know that you have really arrived. This is a qualification rarely awarded to a foreigner, and by no means within the grasp of all the English.

The term describes the sort of behaviour both on and off the playing field that characterises everything they respect. The good sport will play without being seen to be too serious. He will then be dismissive of his victory and magnanimous towards the loser.

> **❝ The term 'a good sport' characterises everything the English respect. ❞**

The good sport will also be a good loser. There will be no arguing with umpires or outward signs of disappointment. On the contrary, a remark such as 'The best man won!' tossed airily to all and sundry is obligatory even in the face of crushing defeat.

This does not mean the English aren't fiercely competitive. Far from it. They would rather be crossed in love than beaten on the tennis court. But to let their disappointment be seen would be 'going too far'.

Equally, to show delight in winning would be seen as 'showing off'. It is not easy being English.

Stoicism

Stoicism, the capacity to greet life's vicissitudes with cheerful calm, is an essential ingredient of Englishness. It is not unfeeling woodenness, fatalism or gloom. It is the trait that enables English people to spend long, wearying hours making their way to and from work on a transport system that many third-world nations would be ashamed of and, having arrived, respond to the question 'How was the journey?', with a breezy 'Not so bad, thanks.'

The English will warm to you if you display understated good humour in the face of adversity. You may then achieve

> **66 The capacity to greet life's vicissitudes with a cheerful calm is an essential ingredient of Englishness. 99**

the status of an admirable stoic, such as the circus worker who, having had his arm bitten off by a tiger was admitted to hospital, and when asked the standard question before treatment 'Are you allergic to anything?', replied 'Only tigers'.

A religious streak

The English are not a deeply religious nation so it is in reality quite a thin streak. They decided that Roman Catholicism with its teachings about original sin and the unworthiness of the human race could not really have been meant for them. So they created a church of their own – the Church of England.

Attendance at Church of England services is not obligatory and, indeed, not a widespread habit. Membership, on the other hand, is assumed to be the norm, and any bureaucratic form which requests information about your religion mirrors the attitude of the nation to the rest of Christendom in its instruction: 'If not C of E, state 'Other'.'

A puritan streak

In general, the English are one of the least introspective of peoples and do not take soul-searching seriously. This doesn't prevent them from brooding every now and then, usually after a major sporting defeat or several weeks of continual rain. But what they do have is a strong puritan streak which runs so deep that few are aware of it.

> **66 The English are one of the least introspective of peoples and do not take soul-searching seriously. 99**

Winning a fortune instead of earning it is one example. Having debated for decades whether or not to have a national lottery, they now debate about whether or not the prizes should be quite so large. There is, they feel, something faintly indecent about people being able to win such huge amounts of money all at once, and that it would be only fair and decent if the person who has won a huge sum would spread it about a bit.

They also worry about moral standards on television and have a 9 p.m. watershed after which the children ought not to be around to be corrupted by explicit sex, bad language and violence – all the things, in fact, that their 13-year-olds get up to in the playground.

> **66 English puritanism is best expressed in the belief that if something is unpleasant, it must be good for you. 99**

English puritanism is best expressed in the belief that if something tastes good it must be bad for you; and if it's unpleasant, it must be good for you. There can be no other explanation for the existence of tapioca pudding.

A practical streak

The bounds of English inventiveness and resourcefulness have yet to be discovered. The garden sheds of England are abuzz with creativity as men called Ron dream up useful and much-needed devices, such as the perfect egg timer, the self-creasing trouser or a little ladder that hangs over the edge of the bath to let the spider out. An Englishman called Babbage was indulged by his friends while he tinkered endlessly with his 'mechanical calculating engines'. The result has revolutionised the modern world – computers.

There is some loss of pride in asking for help or in

not being able to solve your own problems. Initiative is therefore compulsory and is used long before resorting to reading the instructions, calling in the washing machine repairer or borrowing the neighbour's mower.

Clubs and societies

Individuality is all very well, and in some cases commendable, but on the whole being part of a team is important to the English and they are never happier than when they are surrounded by a group of people with whom they either have, or affect to have, everything in common.

> **English life is enriched with clubs and societies, many of which appear to have no sensible or productive purpose.**

English life is enriched with clubs and societies many of which have no sensible or productive purpose to people who are not members – which reinforces the image of the members as individuals. Take the fictional Pickwick Club in Charles Dickens's book; a group who were devoted to dining, telling stories, and going on little journeys. Or the Anti-Caravan Club which was formed as a joke to enable those who disliked caravans to feel they were not alone, and which at one time had more members than its allegedly useful, pro-caravanning counterpart.

If you want to impose free-market policies on the

nation, knock on the door of the Carlton Club. Lovers of buttons have the British Button Society, fans of junk head for the Ephemera Society. If you feel the need to protect the English language, try the Society for the Prevention of Inadvertent Transatlanticisms (SPIT). There are even temporary situation-based clubs where a train full of people will turn into the Signal Failure Club at a moment's notice, given the right circumstances.

Whatever their stated purpose, all English clubs are primarily social groupings whose members take comfort

> **66 Lovers of buttons have the British Button Society, fans of junk head for the Ephemera Society. 99**

in being able to relate to each other without actually having to. Membership assures them human warmth, support, bonding, comradeship and group identity – all with the very English guarantee that, should they happen to meet away from their club gatherings, none of the members need get involved in the others' lives, or even acknowledge the others' existence.

Class

The importance of the class system remains central to the way of life of the English. Dismiss entirely any denials they may give about it not affecting them personally. This just means the individual is comfortable within the class to which he or she has been assigned. Their class is the largest club to which they belong.

There is the highly visible 'official' class system with carefully defined tiers that go from Dukes, Marquises and Earls, to mere commoners who by their own accomplishments have been upgraded with knighthoods and public awards. It is very classy to have all those letters behind your name, such as KG, OBE, BO & RIP.

> **66 The English generally believe that one should marry within one's own peer group. 99**

In fact the system has less real influence than might be supposed. Those at the top end of the scale are usually reluctant to make a big deal of it, because that would be 'showing off', while those nearer the bottom are usually at pains to show how unimpressed they are by the whole thing, as befits good individualists.

Among the upper classes, respect is reserved for old-established families irrespective of titles, or the lack of them. At the other end of the scale, there is a sort of reverse snobbery about being working class. It used to be the proletarian dream to become middle class and drop all working class connections. This has gone into reverse and to be working class has real cachet.

Karl Marx spent years in England writing about 'class war', but never grasped that the real struggle is not between the English upper, middle, and working classes but within them. The struggle is at its fiercest within the biggest section which is the middle class, which has in turn divided itself into an upper, middle and lower class. However, with every year that passes, the divisions get more blurry around the edges.

Although they firmly assert that greater social mobility is desirable, the English generally believe that one should marry within one's own peer group. It saves arguments over whether or not you are going to relax in your 'sitting room' or your 'lounge', and whether or not that room is going to house a life-size ceramic leopard.

Placing each other

It's a national obsession to be able to 'place' one another. It is vital to avoid making a mistake about someone's social position. If they are not totally sure, they will resort to a fiendish series of social tests.

❝ If they are not totally sure of someone's position, they will resort to a fiendish series of social tests. ❞

Accents can instantly place an individual. A regional drawl is no longer considered the fatal flaw it once was, but what used to be called an 'Oxford' accent or 'BBC' pronunciation can still give advantage to someone with it.

Even more telling than vowel sounds is vocabulary. People will distinguish one another's class by whether they say 'lunch' or 'dinner' at lunchtime, have a 'pudding' or a 'sweet' or 'afters', sit on a 'sofa' or a 'settee', or go to the 'loo' or the 'toilet'. There are a myriad such distinctions which allow one group to assess another.

Manners at mealtimes provide yet another opportunity for categorising. The big divide comes in the

> 66 The big divide comes in the method of holding one's knife and fork. 99

method of holding one's knife and fork. Some hold both firmly with the handles covered by the palm. Others hold them loosely like drumsticks with the handles sticking up. Eating peas in either pose is something that needs watching.

If you pass all the tests and establish your credentials, you may earn a grudging respect in English social circles. Finally, though, the laugh is on you. For if you have really had to try, you have lost. The accused in these trials needs to exercise every care except, perhaps, that of caring too much.

Behaviour

Pets

It is an English saying that a person who likes animals cannot be all bad. The English adore animals – all kinds of animals. They keep them, not for status or to guard their property as other nations do, but for company. Animals, especially pets, are vital to English life because pet-owning is for many English people the closest they ever get to an emotional relationship with another being. They are not always very good at talking to each other, but they excel in conversation with their animals. They touch, hug, cradle, carry and stroke them, and whisper sweet nothings into their hairy ears. Pets accept all this without complaint and consequently enjoy an unrivalled position in English affections.

Cats and dogs, parrots and guinea pigs are excused behaviour which if seen in the children of the household

> **66 For many English people pet-owning is the closest they ever get to an emotional relationship with another being. 99**

would be cause for rebuke. Pets are deemed to be incapable of almost any misdemeanour. So when dog bites man, it is always man's fault, even if he is just a passer-by. The victim may be severely savaged but everyone in the vicinity will sympathize with the owner's disclaimer: 'Fang wouldn't hurt a fly!'

Even the criminal fraternity is smiled upon if it shows kindness to animals. The press reported a story about a couple who emerged from a pub to find that their car had been stolen, but that the thief had carefully transferred their dog to the safety of another vehicle before taking off. No mention was made of the car, but the report concluded: 'The owners of 10-year-old Sadie expressed their gratitude.'

The English, who look on stoically as national health hospitals in run-down metropolitan areas close their wards through lack of support and patients spend time on trolleys in corridors, are comforted by the knowledge that wounded hedgehogs are tenderly cared for in a hedgehog hospital.

One of the reasons the English will never fully trust the rest of the world is that foreigners just don't understand about animals, and go on treating them as though they are somehow less than human.

Families

The English usually take 'the family' to mean the small, nuclear family (rather than the large, extended family of, say, the Italians). Indeed, even the nuclear family may be too big, since divorce, single parenthood, or just remaining single are all on the increase. Clearly the English ideal will be reached when everyone in England is living alone, on their own individual island.

> **66 The English ideal will be reached when everyone in England is living alone, on their own individual island. 99**

Two in five marriages in England end in divorce. Two-thirds of divorced people remarry, and two-thirds of people who divorce a second time go on to marry again. Most then settle down, possibly through sheer exhaustion.

Marriage counselling is popular and works because, being English, their reluctance to discuss personal matters with a stranger finally makes them relate to each other.

Children

The English are fond of their children. That said, they're not passionate about them, as they are about dogs, horses, rabbits, cats and even ferrets or weasles. The trouble is that children are not furry and lack that all-important second pair of legs that makes other mammals so attractive and loveable.

At Christmas and on birthdays parents shower the young with presents (anything for peace) and at other times they just try to contain them, preferring to leave their upbringing to others or letting them rear themselves. Parents see their role as being to train their children to be independent and able to look after themselves as adults. This is quite at odds

> 66 The trouble is that children are not furry and lack that all-important second pair of legs. 99

with cultures where the aim is to raise them as part of a life-long dependant family group. For most, childhood is something to be got over as quickly as possible. To be an English grown-up is reckoned a great and glorious thing. It carries much less responsibility than being an English child.

The Elderly

By the time parents are elderly, their children have long since reduced their contact to no more than one visit a week. The parents are far too independent to ask for help, but eventually neighbours and older relatives will shame the children into providing care. Funds permitting (the parent's or the government's funds), they will be lodged in twilight homes and visited even less frequently.

If parents remain in their own homes and then become 'difficult', it is left to daughters to roster some direct care, and probably to 'take in' mum or dad.

> **To the English, eccentricity is a useful way of coping with the problem of anti-social behaviour in one of their own kind.**

Unrelated elders are treated with a certain degree of respect and, when needed, assistance is politely given. This is always provided – and received – on the clear understanding that no continuing obligation is to be expected.

Eccentrics

To the rest of the world the entire English race is eccentric. To the English themselves, the concept of eccentricity is a useful way of coping with the problem of anti-social behaviour in one of their own kind. So, to a certain extent, the English cultivate the idea of eccentricity as agreeable and even admirable.

Being wealthy or famous is an enormous aid to attaining eccentric status. Thus dotty behaviour, such as Lord Berners' decision to dye his flock of doves a host of pretty colours so that they formed a rainbow when they flew into the air, was met with affection. He was, after all, a Lord. Similarly, suburban residents will put up with the antics of an elderly bag-lady residing in a parked car in their street because in her day she was a famous concert pianist.

> **After sending waves of settlers to various outreaches of the globe, a bit of reciprocity could not be denied.**

Eccentrics are excused *de facto* from many of the conventions of correct English conduct. They are living proof that the rules can be broken. However, they are only tolerated if they are apparently unaware of their own eccentricity. Anything else is, of course, deemed to be 'showing off'.

Immigrants

Immigration came largely as a consequence of empire building. After sending waves of settlers to various outreaches of the globe, a bit of reciprocity could not be denied. The English feel it is only natural that others aspire to live amongst them, and it is only proper to accommodate some. But no-one anticipated the *tsunami* of migrants from Eastern Europe that would arrive in Britain as a result of the E.U. policy of open borders between member states. The English now fret about reciprocation of quite another sort, that of being 'taken over'.

Every large English town has a rich mix of nationalities. Around 6 million (10%) of the U.K. population belong to ethnic minorities, and of these half live in London.

Existing immigrant communities are acknowledged to have improved certain aspects of English life. Chicken tikka masala (invented by resourceful Indian restaurateurs) is the single most popular dish in England, and everyone who values the late-night grocer's shop or the newsagent's on the corner has reason to be grateful to the Mr. and Mrs. Patels who almost invariably run them.

> **The English do not see why any immigrant should expect to be fully accepted days, months or even years after their arrival.**

Nevertheless, the English do not see why any immigrant should expect to be fully accepted days, months or even years after their arrival. If assimilation were too easy it would make a mockery of the thousands of years of immigration it has taken to produce the English themselves.

For their part, immigrants may take some time to understand their hosts. It takes several generations before their attitudes are sufficiently modified to even want to be identified as English.

Manners & Etiquette

Formalities

It is generally believed that the English are more formal than they really are. In fact, in day-to-day contact with each other they are less inclined to formality than the French or the Germans. Table manners, once so complex, are less rigid, save for one commandment: 'Don't even think of touching your knife or fork before the last person is seated' or, as happens in some households, before the last person is served.

> **When it comes to physical contact, the English are still deeply reserved. They are not a tactile people.**

Group introductions are incredibly polite and can last for so long that everyone forgets each other's name so the whole business is likely to begin again. First names are commonly used among colleagues, even on the telephone, before those names have met.

Physical contact

When it comes to physical contact, the English are still deeply reserved. They are not a tactile people. A handshake, when it occurs, is a brief, vigorous affair with no hint of lingering. The standard greeting 'How do you do' and the reply 'How do you do' signal the end of the ritual and hands should be crisply withdrawn from contact. Foreigners who assume that 'How do you do' comes with a built-in question mark and respond accordingly are politely rebuffed.

In greeting an old friend, Englishmen allow themselves to put an arm around the other's shoulder, then almost immediately give the other a couple of taps on the back, a bit like a wrestler's gesture of submission, to show that is enough of that. Women may kiss on one or both cheeks; if they do, the miss-kiss is preferred – the kissers making kissing gestures with appropriate sound-effects in the air in the general region of each other's ears.

> 66 In greeting an old friend, Englishmen allow themselves to put an arm around the other's shoulders. 99

Men may also kiss women in greeting, but only on the cheek. Trying to get a kiss on both cheeks can be risky as most women, only expecting the one, do not turn their heads for the second and receive it full frontally, which can result in the worst being feared – i.e., that it was an intentional ploy – an osculatory rape.

In public places, strenuous efforts are made not to touch strangers, even by accident. If this should occur, apologies are fulsome (but they should never be used as an excuse for further conversation).

Gestures

The use of hand gestures in communication is viewed with deep suspicion. Fluttering hands and supple wrists are seen as signs of theatricality (insincerity), effeminacy or foreign extraction.

People will usually only use hand gestures when they are absolutely necessary, such as for pointing the way. A slight bow of the head indicates acknowledgement of one another and a small wave of the hand at waist level can mean 'no, please, you go first'.

The gesture indicating a forceful suggestion (the 'V' sign) is said to have first been employed by English archers at the battle of Agincourt (1415) when standing just beyond the reach of the enemy's arrows, supposedly to indicate that they still had their bow fingers which, had they been captured, the French would have cut off. Whatever the truth, it's the ultimate replacement for words.

> 66 'Nice' is a quintessentially English word whose meaning can only be divined by its context. 99

Being nice

'Nice' is a quintessentially English word whose meaning can only be divined by its context. Being non-specific and uncontentious, it can be used on any occasion to convey a response generally tending towards non-committal approval of anything from the weather to working practices. Its negative form – 'not very nice' – describes habits as diverse as nose-picking to cannibalism.

The English grow up with 'nice'. As children they are warned off anti-social behaviour with the reprimand 'That's not nice' and by the time they totter into their first conversations, they can use the word with deadly effect. They may even imitate their elders by using a sarcastic tone as a put down: 'That's nice! That's *very* nice!'

Please and thank you

The first rule the English come across at an early age is the importance of saying 'Please' and 'Thank you'. Supplication, gratitude and, most important of all,

> **66 Supplication, gratitude and, most important of all, apology are central to English social intercourse. 99**

apology are central to English social intercourse, which is why people seem to use them endlessly. 'Excuse me', 'I'm sorry to tell you…', 'I'm afraid that…', when apology, regret or fear have nothing to do with it, are all forms of social lubrication which spare others' feelings and make life on a small, overcrowded island a little easier.

It is difficult for outsiders to learn how to wield the vocabulary necessary, but the starting point is to understand that it is almost impossible linguistically to be over-grateful, over-apologetic or over-polite when it comes to the point. Thus, the English man or woman whose toe you tread on will be 'so sorry', presumably for allowing the offending digit to get in your way. He or she will then thank you 'so much' when you stop treading on it.

A lack of profusion in the gratitude or apology department will land anyone in such a situation in the 'not very nice' camp from which there is little chance of escape.

Customs & Tradition

Tradition, to the English, represents continuity, which must be preserved at all costs. It gives them a sense of permanence in an age of change. Like a well-worn jersey with holes in the sleeves, it's the comfort of the familiar. By extension, the word 'traditional' implies that something has stood the test of time on its own merits and should be preserved, such as red pillar boxes, cardigans, Marmite and marmalade, Bank Holidays, privet hedges, swirly-patterned carpets, hot water bottles and Wellington boots.

Ceremony

Ceremony – the outward show of tradition – is something the English are especially good at. On state occasions several large bodies of men from mainly aristocratic families (normally confined to barracks) meet in full dress uniform and do quite a lot of marching about and looking fierce in front of the current monarch. In this they are accompanied by noisy brass bands playing mostly German music.

Because their past is infinitely more glamorous than their present, the English cling to it tenaciously, preserving something not for what it is now, but for what it once was. Judicial horsehair wigs, *Abide With Me* sung very badly before the Cup Final, the Queen's Christmas Broadcast to the Commonwealth, the Boat Race, the Shipping Forecast on the radio, the Last Night of the Proms, all intertwine the ceremonial and the traditional, and bring reassurance.

> **Because their past is infinitely more glamorous than their present, the English cling to it tenaciously, preserving something not for what it is now, but for what it once was.**

Yet the English also yearn for change. Not revolutionary change (too noisy) and not anarchy (too extreme); rather, what they long for is to find another way of doing things that is every bit as traditional as the old way. A bright new tomorrow bathed in the warm glow of yesterday is what they aim for; and every so often they bend their collective will towards finding a new way of keeping things fundamentally the same.

Family gatherings

Though they are the least family-orientated people on earth, the English would not dream of spending their Christmas anywhere else but among the bunch of people they refer to as the 'bosom of the family'. This annual merry-making almost always ends in tears and to get over it takes many families a good six months. But tradition rules and, come October, the whole population is beginning to plan for another family Christmas, having apparently completely forgotten the mayhem of the one before.

Christmas apart, family members manage to avoid each other fairly successfully throughout the year except on compulsory occasions such as christenings, weddings and funerals. Of these, christenings and funerals, being the shortest, are the most popular. Weddings are something to be 'got through'. Planning for these events starts early, as do the arguments. Etiquette books crowd the bookshops detailing

> **66 Family members manage to avoid each other fairly successfully throughout the year except on compulsory occasions. 99**

who is responsible for organising and paying for the bride's dress, the flowers, the church, the choir, the organist, the cars, the reception, the food, the photographers and St. John's Ambulance. Every single issue will be chewed over for months, right up to the fateful day, and even after it.

It came as no surprise to many survivors of similar occasions to read the newspaper report of the bride's father who initiated legal proceedings against his son-in-law's parents about who should pay what while the happy couple were still on their honeymoon.

It is the triumph of English hope over English experience that these family gatherings ever take place at all.

Guy Fawkes

On 5th November the English let off fireworks and make bonfires of vast piles of wood, discarded furniture and rubbish in order to burn the effigy of someone who tried to blow up the Houses of Parliament in 1605. Guy Fawkes' foiled attempt is celebrated not because he was discovered before he could kill the King (who was hugely unpopular), but because he had the audacity to try to bring about a change.

Obsessions

The French regard obsession as the necessary precondition of all creativity (and crucial to being a good lover). For the Germans it offers proof of professional ability, staying power and earnestness. For the English, obsessions properly belong to one's leisure hours, and any signs of intellectual or work-related obsession are viewed as indicating a life out of balance. Approved obsessions include:

Homes…

An Englishman's home is his castle. It may be a stately home, a 'two-up, two-down' suburban semi, or just a bedsit, but to the English it is 'hearth and home', the centre of life.

When you visit an English home you will be taken on 'the tour'. This is a lengthy and detailed examination of your host's

> **English homes are in a regular state of siege because of 'improvements'.**

dwelling, concentrating especially on the improvements she or he has made in recent times ('…and here's the new ball valve I've just fitted to the downstairs lavatory. I thought its remarkable performance figures justified the extra expense…').

Inside and out, the occupants busy themselves hanging new wallpaper, tiling showers, assembling furniture and turning the exterior of a little suburban house into a gothic nightmare of mullioned windows, stone-clad walls and studded front doors (they dearly love anything that purports to be something else).

English homes are in a regular state of siege because of 'improvements'. Typically, these improvements knock thousands of pounds off the market value of the property and may plunge the whole neighbourhood into a downward spiral, but they will be your host's pride and joy.

Because the English love DIY so much, English plumbers, carpenters, plasterers and electricians have to be called in at some point to put things right. They form a strutting elite who are in such demand that their hourly rates are comparable with those of Madonna, and will generally arrive in a Porsche (several hours late), look at the job and, with a long intake of breath say, 'It's gonna cost ya.'

... and gardens

The English are most at home in the garden and they truly excel out-of-doors. Gardening is a national pastime and 'green fingers' a proudly borne deformity.

> **66 In summer, the English apply themselves to the horticultural labours of Hercules. 99**

The first sound of spring is not the song of the cuckoo, but the echo of the unprintable oath of the gardener who discovers that his lawn mower will not start. The primeval shout awakens the mower from its winter hibernation and they are off.

In summer, while other people in the world are sitting outside chatting, the English apply themselves to the horticultural labours of Hercules. They weed monster herbaceous borders, build rockeries, nurture giant marrows for the annual village fête and dead-head their asters.

A dedicated band of enthusiasts cultivate cabbages

and carrots on allotments (small bits of municipally-owned land leased to the gardenless). Some wait half their lives to acquire one of these little plots with their ramshackle sheds, for the pleasure of playing market gardeners all weekend.

Should monotony set in, they will visit someone else's garden, preferably one attached to a stately home. Suitably re-energized they return to their own home via the garden centre where they fill their car boot with plants, implements, plastic pond liners and compost.

> **66 The garden gnome reveals a secretive side of the English character. 99**

Come rain or shine, but mostly come rain, the English mulch and prune their way through the year, rejoicing in the fruits of their labour.

Gnomes

The garden gnome reveals a secretive side of the English character – a reminder not of some pagan past but of a time before the coming of adulthood, the very childhood the English think they have left behind.

In English suburban gardens, like the classical statue in the grounds of great English houses, sits the coarse-fishing gnome wielding his little rod. Whether brightly coloured to recall tales of Noddy and Big Ears, or drab and concealed to pretend indifference, they often come accompanied by fairies and roman-

41

tic garden poetry. Along with an ornamental sundial and an Enid Blyton-type name on the garden gate – 'Bide-a-Wee', 'Kenada' (the home of Kenneth and Ada) or 'Olcote' (Our Little Corner of This Earth), they help to create a private world in which the Englishman is just a great friendly giant.

A nice cup of tea

Whilst other people stiffen their sinews with something stronger, the English constitution merely demands tea. They have imbued it with almost mystical curative and comforting qualities. In moments of crisis, as a remedy for shock or just at a social gathering, someone will suggest tea. It's their most socially acceptable addiction.

> **The English have imbued tea with almost mystical curative and comforting qualities.**

Tea to the average English man or woman usually means Indian tea, served with milk and sugar, and the preference is generally for the strength to be rich and copper coloured.

Whether tea bags or tea leaves are used, tea that is still made in a pot has a prodigious amount of folklore concerning its preparation. First the teapot has to be warmed. The tea, once made, has to be left to stand and brew – but not so long that it becomes 'stewed'. Cold milk is poured into the bottom of each cup and then tea is added either with the addition of hot water or, more normally, 'just as it comes' – neat and strong.

In church halls hired for community events tea is often brewed in vast urns like Russian samovars. It should be approached with caution. The liquid that oozes from these receptacles is best described as 'canteen tea' – the kind that stands up without a cup.

Leisure & Pleasure

Leisure activities share with sport the element of competition so essential to the English way of life. The high-flying executive who plays with model helicopters in the local park is subconsciously waiting for another high flier with similar toys to compete with. The man who cleans his car in a suburban street on a Sunday morning is running a polishing race with his neighbour's every grunting sweep of the chamois leather. Even a peaceful pint in the pub can easily turn into a drinking competition if the right adversary turns up.

> **"Leisure activities share with sport the element of competition so essential to the English way of life."**

Theme parks reign as top pleasure outlets on the simple test-to-destruction principle. The passive consumerism of Disneyland is not for the English. Sensible and cautious they may be most of the time, but in a theme park they reveal themselves as closet thrill-seekers. The ideal self-test is one which offers an experience of skydiving, potholing, bobsleighing and whitewater racing all rolled into one SAS-style assault course. Here, the ancient practice of queuing is indulged to its fullest extent for such delights as Deathdive, Nemesis, Suicide Ride and You Must Be Completely Bonkers To Want A Go On This One.

A close cousin of the theme park is the safari park, an attempt by impoverished aristocrats to keep their creditors at bay by populating their estates with large predatory African mammals and charging people to drive their cars around in the hope of seeing one. Large notices warn visitors to keep their windows shut; most English people respond by leaving them just a little bit open, to allow the possibility of being just a little bit mauled.

> **66 Sensible and cautious they may be, but in a theme park they reveal themselves as closet thrill-seekers. 99**

Sports

Sport forms the arena in which the English let go their reserve, their stoicism and – seemingly – their senses, and can become almost continental in their enthusiasm.

The nation's most popular participation sport is fishing – which the English refer to as 'angling' because it sounds as though some skill may be required to do it. More people fish than play football. On a Sunday morning on the banks of any stretch of water anywhere in England you will find a row of seated men surrounded by plastic tubs of grubs, staring forlornly at their lines. The most exciting thing you will see is when they reach for the thermos flask or packed lunch. If by chance a fish is caught, it will probably be thrown back.

But the English person's true devotion to sport involves watching other people play it, ideally surrounded by snacks.

66 Hard-core supporters will show up in sub-zero temperatures or force ten gales. 99

Watching sport provides a vent for pent-up emotions, as well as the comfort of tribal solidarity. Vast numbers of soccer fans will sit up all night with beer and bags of potato crisps to watch the 44th repeat of a goal being scored. Even if they cannot afford the fees for TV sports channels, they will ensure their children have their team's new strip, however many times it changes and regardless of the cost.

Hard-core supporters will show up in the flesh to barrack the opposition in spectator stands or from touchlines, often in sub-zero temperatures or force ten gales with the ever-present threat of a downpour. Nothing can dampen their ardour.

The average English football fan is inured to failure and even derives a sort of masochistic pleasure from his team's ability to snatch defeat – or if he's lucky, a nil–nil draw – from the jaws of victory. The exception is the Manchester United supporter who expects his team to win everything all the time and whinges bitterly when it doesn't. Manchester United has the biggest following of any football club in the world. Each issue of the club's magazine sells in vast numbers – 30,000 copies in Taiwan alone.

Cricket

'If Stalin had learned to play cricket, the world might now be a better place' claimed an English bishop in 1948. Cricket to the English is not just a game, it is a symbol – a 22-man personification of English beliefs and philosophies. Ignore cricket at your peril. You could be 'on a sticky wicket'. You might then be accused of not having put your 'best foot forward' and of not 'playing a straight bat', both the hallmarks of a bounder.

> **Cricket to the English is not just a game, it is a symbol of English beliefs and philosophies.**

The English invented cricket 750 years ago and are fiercely proprietorial about it. Its laws are passed on among the initiated in a coded language, using phrases like 'square leg', 'bowling a maiden over', and 'waiting for a tickle in the slips'. In the past they took the game all over the world and always won. But gradually other nations' teams have got better at playing the game, until now the English stand a pretty safe chance of being beaten wherever they go.

People who are interested in cricket are passionate about it; those who are not are totally indifferent to it. On village greens and TV screens, groups of men, dressed in white, stand around waiting for something to happen. Watching cricket is like transcendental meditation: your mind slowly empties, your mouth goes slack and you start to drool. When you are completely comatose you will hear, after many hours, a distant cry of ''Owzat?!''

> **66 On village greens and TV screens, groups of men, dressed in white, stand around waiting for something to happen. 99**

Because so little happens in cricket, it is customary to accuse the opposition of having cheated: of tampering with the ball by roughing up the surface (so that it behaves in an irregular fashion); of 'sledging' (i.e., hurling abuse at the batsman so as to put him off his stroke), or of playing too fast for a one-day match. All of which the English vigorously complain is just 'not cricket'.

Rambles

When bad weather threatens, the English abandon the shelter of their homes to trek about on foot. Heavy weather is the ultimate adversary – a worthy and familiar opponent. Wrapped from head to toe in waterproof clothing, they set out on extended hikes, best feet forward, carrying maps in little plastic bags hung around their necks. Up hill and down dale, the English follow vehemently protected footpaths on these route marches which they deceptively refer to as 'rambles'.

> **In summer months they will travel miles to pit their stamina against the worst that nature can throw at them.**

In summer months they will travel miles to such places as the Grimpen Mire or the Lake District where rain is almost assured, to pit their stamina against the worst that nature can throw at them.

So popular are these struggles against the elements that some enterprising individuals offer courses in physical discomfort in remote and inhospitable areas of the country where people pay substantial fees to be assured of a serious challenge. These courses, posing under such romantic titles as 'Survival', are pursued for their perceived character-building qualities. The stiffening of upper lips is guaranteed.

Having a flutter

A day out at the races, particularly in the carnival atmosphere of one of the classic races, such as the Grand National or the Derby, is almost unmitigatedly enjoyable.

By contrast, entering a betting shop produces the same frisson as visiting a speakeasy in 1920s Chicago. The English gaming laws decree that the shameful goings-on inside must not be visible from the street, so the windows are frosted or painted out and the open doorway obscured with plastic strips. The interior is dim and bare, with no tables and nothing to sit on; a narrow shelf at chest height is used to write bets on, and to lean against in gloomy anticipation of their outcome. The floor serves as an ashtray.

> 66 The betting shop is the perfect illustration of the English tradition of taking one's pleasures unpleasurably. 99

The betting shop is the perfect illustration of the English tradition of taking one's pleasure unpleasurably. Disappointment at backing a loser is tempered with relief at not having to go back there to collect one's winnings.

Annual holidays

Traditionally, family holidays were almost always spent in one of the many English coastal seaside resorts where the sea air mingles with the smell of fried fish and chips. Here, shops on the seafront sell buckets, spades, lilos, candyfloss, toffee apples, sticks of rock and risqué postcards.

Many families still have holidays at the English

seaside. Pitching their camps of brightly coloured canvas windbreaks on the beach, they spend days on end determinedly enjoying ice creams in the chilliest of temperatures, and wet sand in everything.

The more worldly and adventurous of the English go to the Continent – somewhere hot and sunny – to sit in someone else's seaside resort. The crush of people clamouring for the limited number of places cheap enough to be attractive ensures sufficient demand for the support of fish and chip shops. Fried food and sea air makes them feel right at home.

66 Fried food and sea air makes them feel right at home. 99

French cuisine or charming little Italian trattorias may beguile some, but huge numbers like to go where they can still have access to shops, amusement arcades and warm beer.

Holidays are the raison d'être of English life. Planning one's holiday begins on the way home from the last one. If, as a visitor, you ever run out of small talk, just ask 'Where are you planning to holiday this year?' and then sit back.

Sex

While other nations celebrate their sexuality, to a greater or lesser extent, the English regard theirs as the enemy within.

The Puritans have a lot to answer for. They drove

the issue underground hundreds of years ago and it has been growing there ever since, quietly choking the flower of English youth and occasionally upsetting the entire garden plan. But instead of ploughing up the whole area, the English have played around with trowels and forks for centuries. This is strange, for they are fearless in their confrontation of almost everything else. In all other matters emotional or psychological, while angels hover nervously on the sidelines, the practical

> **Safer, and perhaps more to English taste, is sexual innuendo. They are entirely happy when they are tittering about sex.**

English rush in, dragging their tea urns behind them, ready to cope. When it comes to sex, however, their attitudes are still characterised by the myths and taboos of less enlightened ages.

The English love to read about sex. Newspapers are full of the bedtime exploits of others and the peccadillos of the famous are a constant thrill. But safer, and perhaps more to English taste, is sexual innuendo. They are entirely happy when they are tittering about sex.

Their sex is not free of class distinction. Tradition has it, for example, that the sign of a gentleman is that he will take his own weight on his elbows and, however intimate the moment, he will always remember to thank his hostess for having him, just as she will thank him for coming.

Sense of Humour

The English have a unique sense of humour. You will hear from them with an absolutely straight face the most outrageously sarcastic and witty observation.

Their humour is more than merely wide-ranging: it has a complexity, surrealistic inventiveness and sophistication unmatched in any other English-speaking culture.

It can be intelligent and ironic, as in *Four Weddings and a Funeral*. It can be smutty in the tradition of Benny Hill or the *Carry On* films. It can be satirical like *Spitting Image*, surreal like *Monty Python*, or pathetic like *Mr. Bean*. And no-one does 'cringe humour' as in *The Office* or *Little Britain* with such devastating effect.

> **In English eyes one may be pardoned for all manner of social sins if one is able to laugh about them.**

In English eyes one may be pardoned for all manner of social sins if one is able to laugh about them. In fact, most of the suspicion the English have of foreigners is due to an inability to understand their sense of humour leading to the assumption that they do not have one.

A common factor is an ability and a willingness to deflate pomposity and pride – in oneself most of all. Nothing cemented the popularity of the late Princess Diana as much as her self-mocking remark that she had been 'dim' at school. The fact that she was willing to say so and laugh about it more than made up for any actual dimness. In England, brains are optional but a sense of humour is compulsory.

In everyday life, especially in the workplace, humour is the balm that makes life bearable. No matter how tired, lame or crude the jokes, how trying or wearisome the pranks, it is advisable to laugh like a drain lest you be marked down as serious or – much worse – taking yourself too seriously.

> **❝ In England, brains are optional but a sense of humour is compulsory. ❞**

Since the English rarely say what they mean and tend towards reticence and under-statement, their humour is partly based on an exaggeration of this facet of their own character. So, while in conversation they avoid truths which might lead to confrontation, in their humour they mock that avoidance. For instance:

> At dinner in a great country house, one of the guests drinks rather too much wine and, without warning, slumps across the table. The host rings for the butler and when he arrives says: 'Smithers, could you please prepare a room. This gentleman has kindly consented to stay the night.'

English humour also celebrates weakness and vulnerability with self-deprecation as a way of estab-lishing superiority. Many of the nation's popular TV sitcoms are about people who are failures in society's eyes. It's not the failure that makes the comedy, it's the heroic struggle for success. For instance, in the sitcom *Dad's Army*, set in the Second World War, the bumbling amateurism of a group of elderly men and one gormless youth formed as a Home Guard unit to protect their bit of England is entertaining not only

> **The English are so secure in their self-regard that they can happily poke fun at themselves.**

because they are convinced they are invincible (and therefore more than a match for the ruthless professionalism of the Germans), but because somehow they manage to persuade the audience that, in the event of invasion, they will be.

The English are so secure in their self-regard that they can happily poke fun at themselves. Should you complain about some aspect of English life that is really awful, they will gleefully add stories of trains that never arrive, of bureaucratic bungling that has driven honest citizens to suicide, or of food so disgusting even a dog wouldn't eat it (well, not an English dog).

English humour is as much about recognition as it is about their ability to laugh at themselves, for example: 'I thought my mother was a rotten cook, but at least her gravy used to move about a bit.'

The wry smile that greets the well-judged understatement is a characteristic English expression. They love irony and expect others to appreciate it too. For example:

> First hill walker: 'It's only six miles by the map, yet your navigation made it ten.'
> Second hill walker: 'Yes, but doing it in ten gives one a much greater feeling of accomplishment.'

The English love witty word-play – especially when it's very silly – and they take to

> **66 The English love witty word-play – especially when it's very silly. 99**

their hearts comedians who deliver (with a dead pan expression) jokes of this sort:

'You know, somebody actually complimented me on my driving today. They left a little note on the windscreen which said 'Parking Fine.' So that was nice.'

'The police arrested two youths yesterday. One was drinking battery acid, the other was eating fireworks. They charged the first one and let the other one off.'

'Two cannibals are eating a clown. One says to the other 'Does this taste funny to you?'

A man walked into the doctor's surgery. The doctor said, 'I haven't seen you for a long time.' The man replied 'I know, I've been ill.'

Health & Hygiene

The National Health Service, which makes hospital and medical care virtually free, does away with the English reluctance to seek attention. The waiting lists may be long, but due to the healthcare, life expectancy for men is 78 and women 82 years of age.

There is one perennial national fixation. The French may be fascinated by their livers, the Germans by their digestive systems and the Spanish by their blood, but to the English, none of these have anything like the appeal of the bowels.

> **❝ Kept reasonably steady on home ground, English bowels suffer exquisitely abroad. ❞**

The day that does not start with a satisfactory visit to the lavatory starts on the wrong foot. It is a lifelong preoccupation. While their Continental neighbours breakfast on pastries and jam, the English tuck into bowls of cereal, rich in fibre and advertising their efficacy through such names as 'Force' or 'All Bran'.

Correctives for bowel disorders dominate the bathroom shelves and along with tablets laced with senna, old-fashioned remedies are never entirely left behind. Carter's Little Liver Pills promise to cure 'that out-of-sorts feeling due to constipation'. Syrup of Figs is billed as an effective laxative for all the family. But for the real traditionalist, nothing can beat the vile taste and internal violence of their no-nonsense predecessor, good old-fashioned Castor Oil.

Over-enthusiasm in correcting the effects of being 'bound up' can lead to 'looseness' for which there is yet another array of proprietary medicines designed to bring one back to an acceptably solid state.

Kept reasonably steady on home ground, English bowels suffer exquisitely abroad. Thanks to the dodgy nature of local food and water, the intrepid traveller constantly runs into problems. From Delhi Belly to Montezuma's Revenge or The Aztec Quickstep they strike him or her in every far-flung corner of the earth.

> 66 While the French will even treat a headache with a suppository, the English would rather doctor themselves with potions and prunes. 99

Many juggle with purgatives and binding agents all their lives in the hope of one day returning to that blissful childhood state when an adult would nod approvingly at the first droppings of the day. For them this fæcal nirvana is never reached. None of them can be persuaded to flirt with the ubiquitous suppository so beloved of the Europeans. While the French will even treat a headache with one, the English would rather doctor themselves with potions and prunes.

With more serious illnesses, the English are at their most stoic. Fortitude in the face of adversity is the thing. Queen Victoria's dying words were: 'I feel a little better…'

Hygiene

When it comes to hygiene, the English are traditionally inclined. Showers are gaining in popularity but in most houses the bath still reigns supreme. Here they will happily wallow in their own dirt, diluted with warm, soapy water.

The average household gets through more soap and deodorants than any other European nation. This, as far as they are concerned, counts for a lot. For as every English person knows, other nations, especially the French, just put on more scent when they start to smell.

Eating & Drinking

The English have always been, culinarily speaking, unadventurous and the traditionalist's backlash is ever present. On the whole, 'good plain cooking' and 'honest simple fare' is what's wanted. This carries the clear implication that complicated and pretty dishes are neither good nor honest.

66 'Good plain cooking' and 'honest simple fare' is what's wanted. 99

The writer Somerset Maugham once observed that one could eat very well in England simply by having breakfast three times a day. Although the great English home-cooked breakfast – a sizzling feast of bacon, eggs, sausages, grilled tomatoes, mushrooms, kidneys, kippers, and so on – has given way to a belief that instant coffee and cornflakes must be healthier, it is available 24 hours a day at motorway service stations.

Roast beef, lamb or pork with vegetables and roast potatoes are still the nation's favourite choice for a

> **When inspiration fails, the English fall back on their other traditional dish, baked beans on toast.**

'proper meal'. At all other times, and when inspiration fails, the English fall back on their other traditional dish, baked beans on toast.

The average person gets through 100 kilos of potatoes every year. Mashed potatoes are one of the compulsory three vegetables with each meal. Potatoes also come in the form of crispy snacks and, of course, chips. Fish & chips, Burgers & chips, Steak & chips, Sausages & Chips, Egg & chips or just chips on their own with salt, vinegar and tomato sauce. They are even enjoyed in the form of 'chip butties' – chips stuffed between two halves of a buttered bun.

They also love puddings. Most of the English wouldn't consider a meal finished unless they had a pudding – steamed jam roll, rhubarb crumble, apple pie, treacle pudding, strawberry tart, all the traditional dishes purchased straight from the freezer cabinet. The unwary should take care with 'Yorkshire' and 'black' puddings. Neither is quite what it seems. The first is baked batter eaten with roast beef, and the second a ferocious blood sausage.

As the interest in foreign food has grown, so have the choices. Yet ask the English about restaurants and they talk about the speed of the service, the size of the portions and the price – before, if it is mentioned at all, the meal itself.

In spite of their tastes becoming more sophisticated, the English treasure the sandwich. They are also happy to use up their left-overs. 'Shame to let it go to waste' they chorus. While the French will consign the remains of an evening meal to the bin, the English will eat theirs next day for lunch. They even make a virtue of old cold potatoes and cabbage, serving them, fried, as 'bubble and squeak'.

> **66 Only in England would an Indian restaurant happily sell chips with curry sauce. 99**

English taste is insidious. It assimilates all who come into contact with it. Only in England would an Indian restaurant happily sell chips with curry sauce. Only the English would eat them.

The pub

Drinking in England is not centred on the fluid that is consumed. Drinking is used for companionship – even if you are drinking on your own.

English town pubs are being transformed into wine bars or Irish theme pubs. By contrast, the village pub remains the community institution that it has been for centuries. It consists of one bar plus a 'snug' or small restaurant. It is the focal point of local life, a cross between a social club, a citizens' advice bureau and a parliament. Class and social distinctions are left outside.

> **The village pub is the focal point of local life, a cross between a social club, a citizens' advice bureau and a parliament.**

The traditional English pint which once seemed on the brink of extinction has undergone a renaissance. Thanks to the efforts of the Campaigners for Real Ale (a quintessentially English association of individuals devoted to the preservation, encouragement and consumption of traditional brews), a brimming glass of unfizzy, unchilled, hop-scented beer, hand pumped from a wooden barrel in the cellar is increasingly available – in all its glorious regional and local variations.

> **The habit of drinking 'rounds' is responsible for perhaps two-thirds of pub sales.**

The habit of drinking 'rounds' is responsible for perhaps two-thirds of pub sales. It is not the done thing to drink with others without buying your round. The advantage is that only one person needs to leave the group in order to get six drinks instead of six people queuing up individually. The disadvantage is that you can end up drinking six pints when you only came in for one.

Culture

Literature

England is identified as the country of Shakespeare, Milton, Byron, Dickens and Beatrix Potter. But the true culture of today's England is far more associated with pop idols.

Nevertheless Shakespeare is, by common consent, a hero of the human race, a Titan of literature against

> **66 English audiences of all ages reach for the tissues on hearing how Jemima Puddleduck outwits the fox. 99**

whom all other writers in the world over the past 400 years have been measured. The next three are worthy names in most literate households, but it is the work of Beatrix Potter that is best known; for while the others tended to write about people, she wrote about animals.

A mention of Peter Rabbit, Mrs. Tiggy-Winkle and Jeremy Fisher will elicit an immediate response from English audiences, while the agonies of King Lear, Coriolanus and Othello leave the better read of them intellectually stimulated but emotionally stone-cold. Other nations may thrill to Henry V's call to arms at Agincourt or warm to Juliet's tearful pleas to her Romeo, but English audiences of all ages reach for the tissues on hearing how Jemima Puddleduck out-wits the fox, adjusts her bonnet and escapes the cooking pot to live another sunny day.

Close on the heels of Beatrix Potter comes A.A. Milne, whose *Winnie-The-Pooh* – written by an adult for other adults but passed off as a children's book – is read and re-read by adults for the rest of their lives.

Classical works and a wide selection of good books are regularly read on BBC's Radio 4 – which is considered by many as the

> 66 The English treat their literary legacy as they treat their best tea service: it's nice to know it's there, but perhaps it's best saved for special occasions. 99

last bastion of England's cultural heritage. It also features hugely popular light-hearted programmes where the English pit their wits against one another to amuse the listener with their skill with words.

By and large, the English cherish their literary legacy mostly by ignoring it. They treat it as they treat their best tea service: it's nice to know it's there, but perhaps it's best saved for special occasions.

Television

Television is the closest most English people get to culture. Audiences today complain that programmes are being dumbed down to appeal to the masses and that even the state-run BBC which does not require to make profit has succumbed to the ratings fever that dominates American TV. What is probably most embarrassing for the English is that American-made shows are more popular than their own.

Television on all channels majors in sports coverage and heroic struggles occur between television companies to win exclusive rights to televise the most popular events. But even the English cannot quite live by sport alone. Pandering to the competitive nature of their audiences, broadcasters screen large numbers of quiz and games shows, a wealth of news and discussion programmes and the occasional original excellent drama and wild-life series.

> **66 Heroic struggles occur between television companies to win exclusive rights to televise the most popular sports events. 99**

These are bulked out with comedies, mini-series, reality shows and soaps. The nation is addicted to soaps. It is said that even Her Majesty the Queen watches *Coronation Street* (perhaps attracted by the name).

For the rest, it is old films of which the nation never tires. Programmes aimed at the more intellectual members of society are screened late at night so as to cause the least inconvenience to the majority.

The arts

It has been wisely observed that the English do not much like music but that they do love the noise it makes. This sums up the English attitude to practically all the arts. They are vaguely in favour, so long as they do not have to think about them too much.

They will tolerate ballet as long as it is *Swan Lake* or *The Nutcracker*, and opera so long as it is tuneful like *Carmen* or *La Traviata*. They dislike modern art, but enjoy proclaiming how much they dislike it, so much so that contemporary British artists can earn a living simply by being controversial.

> **The English are vaguely in favour of the arts so long as they do not have to think about them too much.**

They prefer American films to their own, but every year the obligatory quirky British comedy about a bunch of losers will break through. While Hollywood promotes the message that everyone ought to be rich and beautiful, England has cornered the market in films which suggest that people tend to be anything but, and that life is generally a bit of a disappointment. No other country could make such a success out of *Brassed Off*, or *The Full Monty*. Nobody can do failure and laugh at it like the English.

> **England has cornered the market in films which suggest that life is generally a bit of a disappointment.**

The only art form that arouses real emotion among the English is musicals. These the public will happily pay for. When Lloyd Webber meets Beatrix Potter, nobody will be able to get a seat.

The press

Although inclined by nature to mind their own business (or perhaps because of this trait), the English have a passion for newspapers that go out of their way to mind other people's. The sensational revelations of the private life of a notable person are far more interesting than real news.

Some of the more down-market papers in the quest to boost their circulation interpret 'freedom of the press' as the publishing of newspapers free of anything resembling news.

In England, one's choice of newspaper is a badge of identity, a declaration of where one stands, and an affirmation of political belief – as in this tongue-in-cheek profile of newspaper readers: *The Independent* is read by the people who think they should run the country, *The Guardian* by the people who think they do run the country, and *The Times* by the people who actually run the country. *The Financial Times* is read by the people who own the country, *The Daily Telegraph* is read by people who ran the country 60 years ago and *The Sun* is read by people who don't care who runs the country so long as the female on page 3 has great breasts.

> **❝ In England, one's choice of newspaper is a badge of identity. ❞**

Systems

Public transport

The English take masochistic pride in the unreliability of their public transport. Every year, the railways are taken completely by surprise by the wholly unexpected phenomena known as 'autumn' and 'winter'. Trains are delayed and cancelled due to such freak conditions as 'leaves on the line' and 'snow'. If it is pointed out that snow is not exactly unexpected in England, the explanation will be that it's the 'wrong kind of snow'.

Overall the transport systems are reliable but English nature being what it is, they will focus on the negative. You will hear that buses are invariably late. The only exception is when the passenger arrives exactly on time – in which case it is guaranteed that the bus will have arrived and left two minutes early.

> **❝ Trains are delayed and cancelled due to such freak conditions as 'leaves on the line'. ❞**

The English are an instinctively punctual people, but it is by no means bad form to arrive 15 minutes late. It will be put down automatically to transport problems, and hosts will, in fact, rather expect it.

The not so open road

Almost everyone over the age of 17 either owns or has access to a car and uses it frequently, especially for short journeys in suburban areas. This leads to enormous traffic and parking problems in towns, and to terminal motorway congestion. The average speed in built-up areas is now 11 miles an hour – a speed exceeded a hundred years ago by a horse-drawn carriage. Rather than a criticism, this is a very satisfying return to tradition.

Difficulties are doubled by the halving of available road space at all times by roadworks. Highways are under constant siege as vast stretches are cordoned off behind lines of red and white cones. Whole communities spring up with portable site offices, portable lavatories and car parks of their own as road-menders are joined by men working for the gas, electricity, water, telephone and cable TV companies. More often than not this happens serially. When the last of them folds his tent, it's time for the road-menders to move in again.

> **Difficulties are doubled by the halving of available road space at all times by roadworks.**

Driving on the left is traditional and therefore, to the English, indisputably best. The custom dates back to the time when the horse was the main means of getting about, and you kept to the left so as to leave your sword arm free to defend yourself. Nowadays the right arm is usually extended through the open window to reinforce the helpful hints being offered to other motorists.

On the whole, the English are well-behaved on the roads. They use their horns sparingly and often let other drivers in ahead of them. Punctilious in their observation of traffic signs, they will wait at traffic-light-controlled pedestrian crossings even if there are no pedestrians in sight. If there are

> **66 The English will wait at traffic-light-controlled pedestrian crossings even if there are no pedestrians in sight. 99**

any, they screech to a halt and wait patiently for them to cross. This comes as a surprise to foreigners who are used to blessing themselves on the kerb before scuttling across the road like rabbits.

A good education

The function of the English education system is to keep the children amused and to give parents freedom to be involved in more important activities than child minding.

For those who can afford it, this is best done by sending the young to 'public school' (this is a playful little English joke: public schools are in fact private schools, kept that way by fees expensive enough to keep the actual public out). Here children are able to board for months on end. This is believed by parents to be good for their character – but children soon suspect it is rather more good for their parents.

The real public (which really means public)

schools, the free ones run by the state, only keep the little darlings off the streets for a few hours a day. They seem to serve no other discernible purpose: very little education goes on there, and that which does is largely by accident. The schools are beset by a lack of teachers, equipment, buildings, and, indeed, pupils, who are very wisely playing truant.

Crime, Punishment & Law

The policemen who walk the beat ('bobbies') are portrayed in films as being approachable servants of the public who will always give a civil answer. Surprisingly, this is largely accurate. Unless they are part of special forces they do not carry guns, and their presence on the street is primarily a crime prevention one. They are, however, neither harmless nor naïve and patrol with a two-way radio, a knife-proof flak jacket, a CS spray-can and a ninja-style retractable truncheon.

66 Very little education goes on in school, and that which does is largely by accident. 99

Official figures for reported crime are reassuring. Under 5% of English adults are the victims of theft, and less than 2% of violent crime. But figures for *un*reported crime are less comforting. These suggest, for example, that one-third of the victims of theft, burglary and vandalism don't bother to report the crime as they don't think the police will be interested, or will be able to do anything even if they are.

Much of the emphasis of modern policing is on crime prevention, with great success being claimed for security video cameras in public places. However the perpetrators are equally interested in arrest prevention. Typical of this is the police initiative instigated in Romford, Essex, where anyone convicted of shoplifting was banned from entering the town for 12 weeks.

> **❝ Now and then England's prisons are officially declared to be 'full up'. ❞**

The scheme worked: the number of offences was more than halved. This was good news for Romford, but bad news for neighbouring Upminster – where traders reported that shoplifting had doubled.

Prison

Criminal conviction is also successful, so much so that the nation has too many prisoners. Its cramped and crumbling prison system is overloaded. Reforms such as the installation of lavatories in cells that put an end to the practice known as 'slopping-out' have improved matters, but the overcrowding remains. Now and then England's prisons are officially declared to be 'full up'. The last time this happened redundant ships were pressed into service to act as prison hulks – as near as modern sensitivities permitted them to get to the glorious days of old.

Another problem is that people can't decide what prison is for: whether simply to keep bad people out of circulation, or reform them, or give them a really horrible time. The public favours the 'really horrible time' option and reacts indignantly to reports that some well-publicised criminal has got away with community service instead of incarceration, or that prisons are like luxury hotels, or that drugs are more freely available inside than out.

The legal system

The English legal system is a pile of clutter that has accumulated over the centuries. There is no Code of Law, like Napoleon's in France, because the English would never for a moment tolerate a Napoleon. The law, like many aspects of English life, is based on precedent. Everything is decided on what has been done in the past.

> **66 The law, like many aspects of English life, is based on precedent. Everything is decided on what has been done in the past. 99**

An English lawyer will not say, 'This is the Law'. Instead, if you ask, he will say something like 'Well, in 1767, an Act of Parliament said X, but in 1923 a Judge said Y, so my opinion is Z...'

In all criminal cases, the right to be tried before a jury of one's equals forms the basis of Common Law. In such cases, guilt can only be established if proved 'beyond reasonable doubt', otherwise one is assumed to be innocent (or at any rate not criminally guilty). The

> 66 The English like to think that the presumption of innocence shows what a jolly nice, trusting lot they are. 99

English like to think that the presumption of innocence shows what a jolly nice, trusting lot they are. This is all most people know (or care) about their law; the rest is largely impenetrable to the average citizen.

In the criminal courts, the law is acted out as real-life drama in period costume as the judiciary, the guilty and the innocent juggle with truth and false-hood in a courageous attempt to find either; and then, if a prisoner's guilt is established, to make the punishment fit the crime. It is the proud boast of the English legal system that this sometimes happens.

Government

The Constitution

The English like to believe they are ruled by consent. They need to feel that they are the masters of their own fate. They do not take kindly to control of any sort and insist on the fiction that they accept it only on a voluntary basis.

The English Constitution, which formed the bedrock of the British one when the various parts of the United Kingdom were incorporated, is largely an unwritten one. It is based on an accumulation of customs, conventions and laws, that is to say, things happen the way they do because that is the way they always have.

There is no Bill of Rights for citizens. The English say they don't need one. They vigorously defend 'the traditional liberties of an Englishman', but since these too have never been written down no-one knows what they are. However, everyone is still strongly in favour of them, whatever they may be.

> **66 The English vigorously defend 'the traditional liberties of an Englishman', but since these have never been written down no-one knows what they are. 99**

Where other countries give their citizens specific 'rights', the English take a broader view by assuming they have a right to do anything that is not specifically prohibited. After all (as their reasoning goes) having a list of things you can't do leaves plenty of scope for the imaginative person to dream up things the authorities have not got round to making illegal; whereas having a list of things you can do (as in America) leaves the authorities plenty of scope to find reasons for locking you up.

The monarchy

Contrary to the popular belief that supporting a monarch is a hugely expensive business, the British royal family costs each U.K. citizen the price of a KitKat a year – a bargain compared with the expense of supporting (or for that matter, impeaching) a President.

The Monarch is not only the social head, but Head of the Church and titular Head

> **66 Tax demands come in an envelope printed 'On Her Majesty's Service' and even the mail is Royal. 99**

of Government. Tax demands come in an envelope printed 'On Her Majesty's Service' and even the mail is Royal. The head of the monarch on every postage stamp, with no country of origin, is unique to Britain. It is because the system of using pre-paid postage stamps was an invention of the English, who have never been in doubt of their identity.

Respect for the Crown is less than it was, especially among the younger generation, but the monarchy remains personally far more popular than any conceivable alternative.

Government

Now here is an odd thing: England does not have its own Government. It shares a government with Northern Ireland, Scotland and Wales – under the banner of Great Britain.

The idea of 'checks and balances' between the executive Cabinet and the two chambers of the legislature, the House of Lords and the House of Commons, was pioneered by the English. However, this much-copied, much-admired system has been amended in the land of its birth. Power is now concentrated in the hands of the Prime Minister, who nominates the Cabinet. If his party has a majority in the House of Commons, he controls the House rather than the other way around.

> **66 The idea of 'checks and balances' was pioneered by the English. However, this much-copied system has been abandoned in the land of its birth. 99**

He can also nominate peers to the House of Lords. The Lords once included a maverick element of hereditary peers, outside the Prime Minster's control, but a significant number have been evicted in the name of democracy resulting in many peers nominated by the PM and rather less actual democracy.

The discontinuance of the hereditary peers in the House of Lords was met with opposition from inside and outside the House. The public objected because it was a change to the way things have always been done. The hereditary peers objected, not so much because of losing their voting rights, as because of no longer having membership of such a good club.

Local government is in the hands of a complex

network of councils which get 80% of their funding from central government – the other 20% being raised from local property taxes. This 80/20 split is also a fair reflection of the relative influence of central and local government in local affairs.

The only real influence the voters have is to choose which of the two major parties will choose the Prime Minister. The Prime Minister will then choose everything else. This is what is really meant by 'the traditional liberties of an Englishman' – the Englishman in question being the Prime Minister.

Politics

The populace know that politicians are out for their own ends and not to be trusted, yet Ministers are expected to be models of virtue, and if they cannot manage that, they are expected to do the decent thing – resign.

Parliament represents the public in the most English of ways – it does not like change. In a building designed in the

> **66 Parliament represents the public in the most English of ways – it does not like change. 99**

19th century to look 500 years old, the politicians conduct their business with much historical pageantry and partially in period costume.

The political scene is dominated by two parties not called Republicans, Democrats, Solidarity or any other inflated names, but simply Labour and Conservative. It is a little English joke that the Labour Party is now more representative of the middle classes than the labouring classes, and that it is more likely to conserve things than the Conservatives – who are the ones who want to change things. It doesn't matter what the third largest party, the Liberal Democrats, want (even as part of a coalition) because they haven't got much hope of achieving it.

Bureaucracy

The English view bureaucracy – and its associated red tape – as a necessary evil. But, like many other things English, it is perceived as being the best of its kind in the world – and definitely boulevards ahead of anything the rest of Europe has to offer.

Business

Because of their inherent resistance to change it can hardly be a surprise that the English trail the leading industrialised nations in research and development expenditure. They get by with how it has been done in the past more so than the others. It is generally felt that if a method has not originated in England it should be distrusted, so the English will test, discuss, examine and observe it extensively before committing to a sample trial.

Muddling through

Business is characterised by a devotion to democracy. Almost all decisions are taken by committee. Whenever you try to get hold of anyone, you will be told that he or she is 'in a meeting'. They prefer consensus to pragmatic decision making, a compromise that satisfies all egos and is preferable to best practice.

Companies are largely organised on traditional lines – a vertical chain of command from the Chairman and Managing Director at the top, to the humblest employee at

> **Almost all decisions are taken by committee. Whenever you try to get hold of anyone, you will be told that he or she is 'in a meeting'.**

the bottom. You show respect to those above you, friendship for those level with you and disregard for those below you. A survey of university graduates found that those from independent (private) schools still get better-paid jobs than their state-educated contemporaries. The traditional 'old boy' network may be shaken, but it remains unstirred.

The popularly held belief by the English that they work harder than other people took a hammering when a report showed that, on average, the Germans work 44.9 hours a week, the Italians 42.4 and the English 42. The English pointed out that both the Germans and the Italians have more holidays and

> **English people pride themselves on their ability to 'muddle through'.**

that, anyhow, it is not the quantity but the quality of work that counts. They promptly set about discussing the formation of a committee to investigate the possibility of surveying the quality of the output.

English people pride themselves on their ability to 'muddle through', that is, to act without too much worry about discipline or planning. In the past this attitude has served them well, and the past holds all the lessons the English are prepared to heed.

Time keeping

The English admire punctuality and aim for it, but often miss. Their time can be measured in very small amounts: 'Half a mo' is smaller than 'just a sec' but not quite as small as 'in a tick'. On the other hand, 'hang on a minute' can mean anything up to five or six, and 'give me five minutes' usually means around 15.

Public clocks throughout the land enjoy the freedom of living in a democracy of stubborn individualism, with each one giving its own approximation of the same quarter hour.

Just obeying orders

In the same way that an Englishman follows the law only when he chooses to, he follows only those orders that he chooses to.

Orders have therefore to be given with a degree of politeness and indirectness which many other nations will find incomprehensible.

> **Orders have to be given with a degree of politeness and indirectness which many other nations will find incomprehensible.**

Should you receive a request to do something from a person more senior to you, you are meant to treat it as an order. If you, in turn, express an order as a request for a favour you will achieve the desired effect. If you express it simply as an order, with no hint of personal choice, you will find that the English will break for tea.

Language

To the English, language is much more than a means of communication – it is a cultural heritage, something to be held up for display and treasured and admired for its own worth.

While they are inordinately proud of their language, most of them use only a tiny part of it (and then often badly). The *Complete Oxford Dictionary* runs to 23 volumes and contains over 500,000 words. German, on the other hand, has a vocabulary of about 185,000 and French fewer than 100,000. Shakespeare had a working vocabulary of 30,000 words (some of which he invented), twice that of a modern, educated English person. Most of the English manage with around 8,000 – the same as the King James Bible.

> **❝ Shakespeare had a working vocabulary of 30,000 words. Most of the English manage with around 8,000. ❞**

English began as a basic means for various tribes to communicate with each other without all the fuss of gender and inflections. The secret of its international success is that it has shown respect for all other languages by adopting bits of theirs. As someone remarked, 'The English language leads other languages up dark alleyways and then mugs them for all their good words'. For example: 'pyjamas' from Urdu, 'nosh' from Yiddish, 'sofa' from Arabic, 'waltz' from German, 'cinema' from Greek, 'caravan' from Persian, 'bog' from Gaelic, 'shampoo' from Hindi, 'nitwit' from Dutch, 'liaison' from French, 'anorak' from Inuit. Significantly, no other language has so many different ways of saying the same thing.

> **❝ The English language leads other languages up dark alleyways and then mugs them for all their good words. ❞**

The English approve of the tradition of changes of usage within the language while at the same time disapproving of change itself – until they get used to it and regard it as Standard English. They like to dispute spelling and correct usage ('compare with' or 'compare to'), pronunciation ('controversy', 'harass'). It's a game they take seriously.

Meanwhile English is to communication what Microsoft is to computing: unavoidable. The French may insist that English is only used in aviation communication (e.g., Bravo, Golf, Foxtrot) 'pending the development and adoption of a more suitable form of expression', but it soars on regardless. One billion people use it; 80% of the Internet

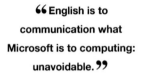

66 English is to communication what Microsoft is to computing: unavoidable. 99

and 75% of the world's mail is written in it, and 200 million-odd Chinese at any given moment are learning it. India has more native English speakers than England has. The Voyager 1 spacecraft in deep space beyond the solar system carries a message from the United Nations on behalf of 147 countries – in English.

It will soon be possible for English people to travel anywhere in the world and speak their own language without having to repeat themselves or raise their voices in an attempt to be understood. It's a prospect which makes them feel – in a word which has no exact equivalent in any of the world's other 2,700 languages or cultures – 'comfy'.

Conversation

Side-stepping

A social conversation with the English is called 'chatting'. When you're chatting, you do not talk about the arts, politics, death, literature, work or anything that you actually believe in. You talk about holidays, animals, the weather, sport or how awful the people on the other side of the room are.

Because they chat in order to side-step serious issues, the English have developed a bewildering battery of metaphors with which everyone is familiar and comfortable. These include

> **To side-step serious issues, the English have developed a bewildering battery of metaphors.**

euphemisms for the avoidance of verbal confrontation with tricky subjects. For example, the English do not die, they 'pass over', 'pass on', 'pop off', 'kick the bucket', 'give up the ghost' or 'snuff it'. When they need to relieve themselves they 'spend a penny', 'wash their hands', 'answer the call', 'make use of the facilities' or, simply, 'go'.

They are devoted to a huge range of hackneyed expressions which they often use to keep the conversational ball in play, or to cover their escape. Because they are slightly ashamed of the triteness of these, they refer to them dismissively, in French, as 'clichés'. Moving from one cliché to another, the skilful user will avoid taking a stance on anything at all.

English weather

Without the conversational topic of the weather, no two English people would ever get to know each other. Commiserating about or marvelling at the weather is the essential conversation-opener without which social intercourse can never get under way.

Rather like the inhabitants, the weather is unpredictable. The geographic location of the country makes it naturally prey to momentary atmospheric changes, and forward planning of any outdoor event is fraught with misgivings. The populace has, of course, lived with this situation for hundreds of years but, not being extreme themselves, extremes in weather conditions always take them by surprise.

> **66 Without the conversational topic of the weather, no two English people would ever get to know each other. 99**

But while late frosts kill cherished plants and cloudbursts wash away the tea tents at village fêtes in high summer, they have, in English eyes, a higher purpose – to furnish conversation. 'Nippy, isn't it?', 'They say it'll be sunny tomorrow', 'Looks like we're in for a cold snap'. Bracing, parky, muggy, breezy, crisp, chilly, fresh – conditions are always understated by at least 10 degrees.

When you can tell the difference between 'scattered showers', 'showery outbreaks', and 'intermittent rain', you'll know you have finally arrived at a state of complete Englishness.

The Authors

Antony Miall (RIP) was born in the Lake District but migrated south at nine months old and spent his childhood in Royal Tunbridge Wells, Kent, where he had ample opportunity to observe the English at their most characteristic.

He spent his life safely in the south, within easy reach of France which suited him very well because he always felt he never quite qualified in Englishness. Among the subjects he was unable to get to grips with were discomfort and moderation. Nevertheless, held in thrall by his two cats, he was obliged to admit to giving way to the thoroughly English tradition of pet worship, fondly recalling a period when he worked in Public Relations and promoted water beds for sensitive dogs.

David Milsted, a typically mongrel Englishman (in his case, one-quarter Scots with trace elements of Viking), was born in the south and subsequently drifted northward, eventually spending 15 years on various Scottish islands before relocating, more or less accidentally, to Dorset, where he, his partner, his four sons and two stepsons constitute a 0.75% typical English family.

A former teacher, fireman and postman, he is now a full-time writer, researcher and editor who makes occasional forays into broadcasting, the theatre, and the strangely beautiful world of corporate malt whisky tasting. He has published four novels and a number of reference books, such as *Brewer's Anthology of England and the English* and *The Cassell Dictionary of Regrettable Quotations*.

———————————

Acknowledgement and thanks are given to Ben Barkow, Ken Hunt and John Winterson Richards for their witty ideas and contributions.

The Swedes

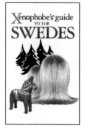

The Swedes brood a lot over the meaning of life in a self-absorbed sort of way, without ever arriving at satisfactory answers. The stark images and unresolved plots in many of Ingmar Bergman's films are accurate snapshots of the Swedish psyche.

The Aussies

Never make the error of underestimating the Aussies. They love to portray a casual disregard for everything around them, but no-one accidentally achieves a lifestyle as relaxed as theirs.

The Italians

Italians grow up knowing that they have to be economical with the truth. All other Italians are, so if they didn't play the game they would be at a serious disadvantage. They have to fabricate to keep one step ahead.

The Americans

The American language embraces the bias towards good feelings. Stocks that plummet to half their value aren't losers, they're 'non-performers'. Someone doesn't have a near brush with death; he or she has a 'life-affirming experience'.

The Germans

The Germans strongly disapprove of the irrelevant, the flippant, the accidental. On the whole they would prefer to forgo a clever invention rather than admit that creativity is a random and chaotic process.

The French

To the French, there is a world of difference between rules and formalities. The former are to be ignored, the latter strictly observed. Everything must be done *comme il faut* (properly), from filling in a form to stuffing a duck.

Comments on Xenophobe's® Guides

On the series:

'Good-humoured support for taking one's first steps toward understanding the foibles of an alien culture.' *Stamford's Travel Guides*

The Estonians:

'Filled with clever observations and self-ironic descriptions that shed light on the Estonian soul, its uniqueness and its phobias.' Estonian reader in Paris

The Welsh:

'Wonderful. The observations of the peculiarities and foibles of the Welsh are highly accurate and I could see myself in almost every paragraph.' Reader from Wales

The Danes:

'I laughed till I cried. After two years in Denmark this book still manages to provide insights into the Danes. I find myself quoting it when trying to describe them to others.' Reader from London

The Poles

'Never have I understood a culture better! Very funny. Worth reading even if you are not going there.' Anonymous reader

Xenophobe's® guides

Available as printed books and e-books:

The Americans	The Kiwis
The Aussies	The Norwegians
The Austrians	The Poles
The Belgians	The Portuguese
The Canadians	The Russians
The Chinese	The Scots
The Czechs	The Spanish
The Danes	The Swedes
The Dutch	The Swiss
The English	The Welsh
The Estonians	
The Finns	
The French	
The Germans	**Xenophobe's®**
The Greeks	**lingo learners**
The Icelanders	
The Irish	French
The Israelis	German
The Italians	Greek
The Japanese	Italian
	Spanish

Xenophobe's Guides

Xenophobe's® Guides e-books are available from Amazon, iBookstore, and other online sources, and via:

www.xenophobes.com

Xenophobe's® Guides print versions can be purchased through online retailers (Amazon, etc.) or via our web site:

www.xenophobes.com

The Publisher is pleased to offer a quantity discount on book orders. Why not embellish an occasion – a wedding goody bag, a conference or other corporate event – with our guides. Or treat yourself to a full set of the paperback edition. Ask us for details:

Xenophobe's® Guides

telephone: +44 (0)20 7733 8585
e-mail: info@xenophobes.com

Xenophobe's® Guides enhance your understanding of the people of different nations. Don't miss out – order your next Xenophobe's® Guide soon.

Xenophobe's Guides